RACE FOR YOUR LIFE!

ANTARCTICA MARATHON

BY KATE MIKOLEY

Gareth Stevens PUBLISHING

HOT TOPICS

Please visit our website, www.garethstevens.com. For a free color catalog of all our high-quality books, call toll free 1-800-542-2595 or fax 1-877-542-2596.

Cataloging-in-Publication Data

Names: Mikoley, Kate.
Title: Antarctica marathon / Kate Mikoley.
Description: New York : Gareth Stevens Publishing, 2021. | Series: Race for your life! | Includes glossary and index.
Identifiers: ISBN 9781538259146 (pbk.) | ISBN 9781538259160 (library bound) | ISBN 9781538259153 (6 pack)
Subjects: LCSH: Marathon running–Juvenile literature. | Running races–Juvenile literature. | Marathon running–Antarctica.
Classification: LCC GV1065.M57 2021 | DDC 796.42'52–dc23

First Edition

Published in 2021 by
Gareth Stevens Publishing
111 East 14th Street, Suite 349
New York, NY 10003

Designer: Laura Bowen
Editor: Kate Mikoley

Photo credits: Cover, pp. 1–32 (texture) Chatham172/Shutterstock.com; cover, p.1 (mountains) Matt Makes Photos/Shutterstock.com; cover, pp. 1 (runner), 25, 27 FRANCK FIFE/ Staff/AFP/Getty Images; p. 5 (map) Peter Hermes Furian/ Shutterstock.com; p. 5 (aerial photo) Alex.Munoz/Shutterstock.com; p. 7 dani3315/Shutterstock.com; pp. 9, 11, 15, 17, 23 AFP/Stringer/AFP/Getty Images; p. 13 Alexey Seafarer/Shutterstock.com; p. 19 JOHAN ORDONEZ/Contributor/ AFP/Getty Images; p. 21 Andrew Mobbs/Shutterstock.com; p. 29 SolStock/E+/ Getty Images.

Printed in the United States of America

CPSIA compliance information: Batch #CS20GS: For further information contact Gareth Stevens, New York, New York at 1-800-542-2595.

CONTENTS

A CHILLY COURSE

Have you ever run a mile? Imagine doing that 26 times in a row! Add an extra 0.2 mile (0.3 km) and you've got a marathon. What could make running that far even harder? Doing it on Earth's coldest **continent**!

FEARLESS FACTS

The Antarctica Marathon takes place on King George Island, about 75 miles (120 km) off the coast of the main part of Antarctica.

The lowest **temperature** ever recorded on Earth was -128.6°F (-89.2°C) in **inland** Antarctica. Luckily, King George Island doesn't get quite that cold. Still, the temperature during the race is commonly between 15°F (-9.4°C) and 34°F (1.1°C).

FEARLESS FACTS

Antarctica isn't just the coldest continent—it's also the windiest. With the wind, temperatures can feel about 10°F (5.6°C) colder than they really are.

When a runner signs up for the Antarctica Marathon, they're never sure exactly what they're going to get. It may snow a lot during the race, just a little, or not at all. The race is held on dirt roads, which are often very muddy!

FEARLESS FACTS

The course, or path of the race, has hills and is often icy. Runners need to train to be able to handle these conditions.

OFF TO ANTARCTICA

Unlike other parts of the world, no one lives in Antarctica all the time. People there are either on a trip, like the marathon runners, or work there for short periods of time. Workers live at stations where scientific research, or studying, is done.

FEARLESS FACTS

The course for the Antarctica Marathon goes by several scientific research stations!

All marathons take a lot of hard work and training. But the Antarctica Marathon isn't like other races. Runners can't just drive to the beginning of the course. In fact, they don't even take a plane there. They take a ship!

FEARLESS FACTS

The ship to King George Island leaves from the southern tip of Argentina. The ride takes more than two days!

SEEING THE SIGHTS

Runners get to see some amazing sights in and on their way to Antarctica. They may see large pieces of ice that float in the sea, called icebergs, and other large areas of ice, called glaciers. Glaciers move slowly over large areas of land.

FEARLESS FACTS

During their trip, runners may get to see animals native to Antarctica, such as penguins, whales, and seals.

WHY RUN?

People run marathons for many reasons. Some want to push how far they can go. Others want to beat their own time record. Antarctica Marathoners certainly push themselves, but beating a record is hard to do in this race. It's not an easy course!

FEARLESS FACTS

People come from many countries to run the Antarctica Marathon. Runners get to meet people from around the world!

Some runners have a goal of running a marathon on all seven continents! Antarctica's the hardest one to get. The Antarctica Marathon was first held in 1995. Today, there are a few other races held in Antarctica, including two in the main part of the continent.

FEARLESS FACTS

Antarctica was the last continent to be discovered. The Antarctica Marathon is sometimes called "the last marathon."

A GOOD CAUSE

Some of the money made from the Antarctica Marathon helps a group called Oceanites. The group researches the effects that **climate change** and visitors have on Antarctica. They study animals and plants in Antarctica to find ways to help the **environment**.

FEARLESS FACTS

Efforts are made to not harm the environment during the race. This is done by limiting, or capping, the number of people allowed to race and making sure no trash is left behind.

GETTING IN

In addition to being a hard race to run, it can also be hard to book a spot in the Antarctica Marathon. Spots often fill up several years in advance! It's also pricey, at more than $5,000 per person!

FEARLESS FACTS

You must be 18 to run the Antarctica Marathon. A half marathon, or 13.1-mile (21 km) run, is open to all ages.

GEAR UP!

Running 26.2 miles (42.2 km) isn't easy, even for the best **athletes**. People often follow training plans to work up to running that far. For races in places like Antarctica, people may train with special gear to get used to running in unusual conditions.

FEARLESS FACTS

For cold races, people commonly wear **waterproof** clothing and special glasses to keep their eyes safe from the snow and cold.

Sometimes, one of the toughest parts about running in the cold is figuring out what to wear! You'll get a little warmer once you start running, but in a place like Antarctica you still need to wear lots of warm clothes.

FEARLESS FACTS

For really cold races, some people train in rooms made to be as cold as the place where the race is held. They'll even practice with their snow gear on!

GET RUNNING!

If you think you may want to run the Antarctica Marathon someday, you can start running now. If your school has a track or cross-country team, try joining. A coach can help you learn how to avoid, or stay away from, getting hurt while running.

FEARLESS FACTS

Practicing with a group is a great way to stay safe and driven while running. Plus, you get to have fun with friends!

GEAR CHECKLIST

Some things you may need to wear during the Antarctica Marathon include:

- WINTER COAT
- WATERPROOF COAT AND PANTS
- WATERPROOF GLOVES
- QUICK-DRYING SHIRT AND SOCKS
- SHOES MADE FOR WET AND MUDDY TRAILS
- WINTER HAT
- PROTECTIVE GLASSES

FOR MORE INFORMATION

BOOKS

Doeden, Matt. *Surviving the Marathon des Sables: An Interactive Extreme Sports Adventure.* North Mankato, MN: Capstone Press, 2018.

Scheff, Matt. *Amazing Human Feats of Distance.* North Mankato, MN: Bright Idea Books, 2019.

Vanden Branden, Claire. *Antarctica.* Minneapolis, MN: Cody Koala, 2019.

WEBSITES

Antarctica
www.nationalgeographic.org/encyclopedia/antarctica/
Learn more about the unique continent where the Antarctica Marathon takes place.

Antarctica Marathon and Half-Marathon
www.marathontours.com/races/antarctica-marathon-and-half-386
Keep up on all the latest news about the Antarctica Marathon here.

How Long Is a Marathon?
www.wonderopolis.org/wonder/how-long-is-a-marathon
Learn more fun facts about marathons and their history here.

GLOSSARY

athlete: someone who is physically fit and takes part in sporting events

climate change: long-term change in Earth's climate, caused partly by human activities such as burning oil and natural gas

continent: one of Earth's seven great landmasses

environment: the natural world in which plants and animals live

inland: toward the middle of an area of land

temperature: how hot or cold something is

waterproof: able to keep water out

INDEX